# It's a
# Girl

summersdale

IT'S A GIRL

An Hachette UK Company
www.hachette.co.uk

Summersdale Publishers Ltd
Part of Octopus Publishing Group Limited
Carmelite House
50 Victoria Embankment
LONDON
EC4Y 0DZ
UK

www.summersdale.com

Printed and bound in China

ISBN: 978-1-78685-788-0

Substantial discounts on bulk quantities of Summersdale books are available to corporations, professional associations and other organisations. For details contact general enquiries: telephone: +44 (0) 1243 771107 or email: enquiries@summersdale.com.

To ..............................

From ..............................

A new baby is like
the beginning of all
things — wonder,
hope, a dream
of possibilities.

EDA J. LESHAN

There is no friendship,
no love, like that of the
parent for the child.

HENRY WARD BEECHER

THE RAISING
OF A CHILD IS
THE BUILDING
OF A
CATHEDRAL.
YOU CAN'T
CUT CORNERS.

**DAVE EGGERS**

I've learned more from my daughter than she has learned from me.

ANTONIO BANDERAS

There is nothing like
a newborn baby to
renew your spirit and
to buttress your resolve
to make the world
a better place.

**VIRGINIA KELLEY**

**There is no kind of affection so purely angelic as of a father to a daughter.**

JOSEPH ADDISON

ALL MY
EGGS ARE IN
ONE BASKET,
AND THAT'S
MY FAMILY.

BLAKE LIVELY

A baby will make love
stronger, days shorter,
nights longer, bankroll
smaller, home happier,
clothes shabbier, the past
forgotten, and the future
worth living for.

You hear people say it all the time, how life changes so drastically. But you can't possibly grasp how beautiful that is until you have your child.

PINK

Sometimes... the smallest
things take up the most
room in your heart.

A. A. MILNE

Love crawls with the baby, walks with the toddler, runs with the child, then stands aside to let the youth walk into adulthood.

JO ANN MERRELL

If you want your children to turn out well, spend twice as much time with them and half as much money.

Govern a family
as you would
cook a small fish
– very gently.

CHINESE PROVERB

What good
mothers and
fathers instinctively
feel like doing
for their babies
is usually best
after all.

BENJAMIN SPOCK

Where there is
great love, there are
always miracles.

WILLA CATHER

**Words cannot express the joy of new life.**

HERMANN HESSE

Nothing is more
important or scary than
protecting a daughter.

CHANNING TATUM

Every child begins
the world again.

HENRY DAVID THOREAU

YOUR
GREATEST
CONTRIBUTION
MAY NOT BE
SOMETHING
YOU DO BUT
SOMEONE
YOU RAISE.

ANONYMOUS

A daughter is
just a little girl
who grows up to be
your best friend.

ANONYMOUS

**A child is an uncut diamond.**

AUSTIN O'MALLEY

Once you bring kids
into the world, it's not
about you any more.

TONY GASKINS

There is absolutely no way
that labour is harder than
installing a car seat.

CHRISSY TEIGEN

I feel more beautiful
than I've ever felt
because I've given birth.

# Children make you want to start life over.

MUHAMMAD ALI

I'M SO
PROUD OF
YOU THAT
IT MAKES
ME PROUD
OF ME.

JOHN GREEN

Success, and even life itself, wouldn't be worth anything if I didn't have my children by my side.

JUDE LAW

There is a special
place in heaven for the
father who takes his
daughter shopping.

JOHN SINOR

CHILDREN
HAVE NEITHER
PAST NOR
FUTURE. THEY
ENJOY THE
PRESENT,
WHICH VERY
FEW OF
US DO.

JEAN DE LA BRUYÈRE

You aren't wealthy until you have something money can't buy.

GARTH BROOKS

No other stranger cares
that your kid ate an
artichoke, but you think
it's the best story ever.

**JIMMY FALLON**

**Kids go where there is excitement. They stay where there is love.**

ZIG ZIGLAR

WHILE WE TRY
TO TEACH OUR
CHILDREN
ALL ABOUT
LIFE, OUR
CHILDREN
TEACH US
WHAT LIFE IS
ALL ABOUT.

ANONYMOUS

I wanted to call my
parents and say, 'I'm sorry,
because I never knew how
much you loved me.'

ASHTON KUTCHER

If it's an oak tree,
I want it to grow
as an oak tree. I'm
not going to try to
force it to be an
apple tree.

**WILL SMITH**

And though she be but little, she is fierce.

WILLIAM SHAKESPEARE

It's a very powerful feeling to see the product of your love right there in front of you.

JOHN LEGEND

If we were ever under
attack, I would use my
wife as a human shield
to protect that baby.

RYAN REYNOLDS

It is the nature
of babies to
be in bliss.

Love is the only
reality and it is not
a mere sentiment.
It is the ultimate
truth that lies
at the heart
of creation.

RABINDRANATH TAGORE

Wrinkles are hereditary –
parents get them from
their children.

DORIS DAY

**I didn't expect babies to need so many diapers.**

SHAKIRA

A daughter may outgrow
your lap, but she will never
outgrow your heart.

ANONYMOUS

Children are the
bridge to heaven.

PERSIAN PROVERB

MY NEW
FAVOURITE
SMELL IS
NEW BABY
SMELL. IT
MAKES ME
SO HAPPY.

JANE KRAKOWSKI

Having a baby
is a life-changer.
It gives you a whole
other perspective on
why you wake up
every day.

**TAYLOR HANSON**

Love for children is perhaps the most intense love.

WERNER BERGENGRUEN

When I come home,
my daughter will run to
the door and give me a
big hug, and everything...
just melts away.

HUGH JACKMAN

All that children need is love, a grown-up to take responsibility for them, and a soft place to land.

DEBORAH HARKNESS

Having a little girl
has been like following
an old treasure map
with the important
paths torn away.

HEATHER GUDENKAUF

# Our household feels overwhelmed with love.

CHRISSY TEIGEN

TO THE
WORLD YOU
MAY BE ONE
PERSON;
BUT TO ONE
PERSON YOU
MAY BE THE
WORLD.

**DR SEUSS**

Children will not remember you for the material things you provided, but for the feeling that you cherished them.

RICHARD L. EVANS

We cannot always build
the future for our youth,
but we can build our
youth for the future.

FRANKLIN D. ROOSEVELT

THERE IS NO
WAY TO BE
A PERFECT
PARENT, AND
A MILLION
WAYS TO BE
A GOOD
ONE.

ANONYMOUS

In the garden
of humanity
every baby is a
fresh new flower.

DEBASISH MRIDHA

Having a
baby dragged me,
kicking and screaming,
from the world of
self-absorption.

PAUL REISER

**She has my feet, which is a bummer for her.**

ADAM LEVINE

CHILDREN ARE THE WORLD'S MOST VALUABLE RESOURCE AND ITS BEST HOPE FOR THE FUTURE.

JOHN F. KENNEDY

The best and most
beautiful things in the
world cannot be seen or
even touched. They must
be felt with the heart.

HELEN KELLER

The hand that rocks the cradle is usually attached to someone who isn't getting enough sleep.

JOHN FIEBIG

You will always be your child's favourite toy.

VICKI LANSKY

A little girl can be sweeter (and badder) oftener than anyone else in the world.

ALAN MARSHALL BECK

Until you have a
baby, you don't even
realise how much you
were missing one.

JODI PICOULT

# In time of test, family is best.

BURMESE PROVERB

You can learn
many things from
children. How much
patience you have,
for instance.

FRANKLIN P. JONES

When they placed you
in my arms, you slipped
into my heart.

ANONYMOUS

**Every baby needs a lap.**

HENRY ROBIN

The most precious
jewels you'll have around
your neck are the arms
of your daughter.

ANONYMOUS

Every beetle is a gazelle
in the eyes of its mother.

MOORISH PROVERB

PARENTS
LEARN A LOT
FROM THEIR
CHILDREN
ABOUT
COPING
WITH LIFE.

MURIEL SPARK

I understood once
I held a baby in my
arms, why some
people have the need
to keep having them.

**SPALDING GRAY**

**Family is not an important thing. It's everything.**

MICHAEL J. FOX

We find a delight in the beauty and happiness of children that makes the heart too big for the body.

RALPH WALDO EMERSON

A daughter is a miracle
that never ceases to
be miraculous.

DEANNA BEISSER

Your children need
your presence more
than your presents.

JESSE JACKSON

# A happy family is but an earlier heaven.

GEORGE BERNARD SHAW

LIFE DOESN'T
COME
WITH AN
INSTRUCTION
BOOK; THAT'S
WHY WE HAVE
PARENTS.

ANONYMOUS

Loving a baby is a
circular business...
the more you give
the more you get.

PENELOPE LEACH

Birth is an experience that
demonstrates that life is
not merely function and
utility, but form and beauty.

CHRISTOPHER LARGEN

MY
DAUGHTER
JUST MAKES
ME HAPPY,
AND SHE
MOTIVATES
ME TO BE A
KID AGAIN.

**CHRISTINA MILIAN**

# Happiness is only real when shared.

ANONYMOUS

Children must be
taught how to think,
not what to think.

MARGARET MEAD

A child is not a vase
to be filled, but a
fire to be lit.

FRANÇOIS RABELAIS

OTHER
THINGS MAY
CHANGE
US, BUT WE
START AND
END WITH
THE FAMILY.

ANTHONY BRANDT

My daughter is the
funniest person I know,
and I couldn't imagine
my life without her.

DONNA AIR

To witness the birth
of a child is our
best opportunity
to experience the
meaning of the
word 'miracle'.

**PAUL CARVEL**

It takes courage
to raise children.

JOHN STEINBECK

Everything in our
life should be
based on love.

RAY BRADBURY

Allow children to be happy
in their own way, for what
better way will they find?

SAMUEL JOHNSON

The soul is
healed by being
with children.

FYODOR DOSTOEVSKY

Raising a young lady is a mystery even beyond an enchanter's skill.

LLOYD ALEXANDER

Before I got married I had
six theories about bringing
up children; now I have six
children and no theories.

JOHN WILMOT

**Children learn
to smile from
their parents.**

SHINICHI SUZUKI

There are only two lasting bequests we can hope to give our children. One is roots. The other is wings.

HODDING CARTER

Children make your
life important.

ERMA BOMBECK

I SUSTAIN
MYSELF
WITH THE
LOVE OF
FAMILY.

MAYA ANGELOU

I love to think that the day you're born, you're given the world as your birthday present.

LEO BUSCAGLIA

**Raising kids is part joy and part guerrilla warfare.**

ED ASNER

A toddling little
girl is a centre of
common feeling
which makes the
most dissimilar
people understand
each other.

GEORGE ELIOT

Pregnancy is a process
that invites you to
surrender to the unseen
force behind all life.

JUDY FORD

Children are a great
comfort in your old age
– and they help you
reach it faster, too.

ANONYMOUS

Every child is
one caring adult
away from being
a success story.

JOSH SHIPP

THE BEST
MUSIC I
HAVE EVER
HEARD IS
THE SOUND
OF MY
DAUGHTER'S
GIGGLING.

**DEBASISH MRIDHA**

Each day of our
lives we make
deposits in the
memory banks
of our children.

CHARLES R. SWINDOLL

A baby is something you
carry inside you for nine
months, in your arms for
three years and in your
heart till the day you die.

MARY MASON

A PERSON
SOON LEARNS
HOW LITTLE
HE KNOWS
WHEN A
CHILD BEGINS
TO ASK
QUESTIONS.

RICHARD L. EVANS

No act of
kindness, no
matter how small,
is ever wasted.

Even when freshly
washed and relieved
of all obvious
confections, children
tend to be sticky.

**FRAN LEBOWITZ**

We never know
the love of the
parent till we become
parents ourselves.

HENRY WARD BEECHER

THE RULES
FOR
PARENTS
ARE THREE...
LOVE, LIMIT,
AND LET
THEM BE.

ELAINE M. WARD

When you are dealing
with a child, keep all
your wits about you,
and sit on the floor.

AUSTIN O'MALLEY

A little girl is
sugar and spice
and everything nice
– especially when
she's taking a nap.

**ANONYMOUS**

Hugs can do great
amounts of good –
especially for children.

PRINCESS DIANA

The gain is not the
having of children; it
is the discovery of love
and how to be loving.

POLLY BERRIEN BERENDS

Never let a problem
to be solved become
more important than a
person to be loved.

THOMAS S. MONSON

Children see
magic because
they look for it.

CHRISTOPHER MOORE

There's no road map on how to raise a family: it's always an enormous negotiation.

MERYL STREEP

Act as if what
you do makes a
difference. It does.

WILLIAM JAMES

**What is a home without children? Quiet.**

HENNY YOUNGMAN

Getting a burp out of your
little thing is probably
the greatest satisfaction
I've come across.

BRAD PITT

A perfect example
of minority rule is a
baby in the house.

ANONYMOUS

DON'T EVER
TELL THE
MOTHER OF
A NEWBORN
THAT HER
BABY'S
SMILE IS
JUST GAS.

ANONYMOUS

You have a lifetime to
work, but children are
only young once.

POLISH PROVERB

**Everything depends
on upbringing.**

LEO TOLSTOY

Little girls are the
nicest things that
can happen to people.
They're born with
a bit of angel-shine
about them.

ALAN MARSHALL BECK

Our greatest natural
resource is the minds
of our children.

WALT DISNEY

The child supplies the power but the parents have to do the steering.

DR BENJAMIN SPOCK

A daughter is a
day brightener
and a heart
warmer.

ANONYMOUS

A DAUGHTER
IS A
TREASURE
– AND A
CAUSE OF
SLEEPLESSNESS.

**BEN SIRA**

Always kiss your children goodnight, even if they're already asleep.

H. JACKSON BROWN JR

A parent is someone
who carries pictures in
their wallet where their
money used to be.

ANONYMOUS

YOU
CANNOT BUY
HAPPINESS.
HAPPINESS
IS BORN.

**ANONYMOUS**

# Do all things with love.

OG MANDINO

Making a decision
to have a child –
it's momentous. It
is to decide forever
to have your heart
go walking around
outside your body.

**ELIZABETH STONE**

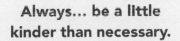

**Always… be a little kinder than necessary.**

J. M. BARRIE

PEOPLE
WHO SAY
THEY SLEEP
LIKE A BABY
USUALLY
DON'T HAVE
ONE.

LEO BURKE

It goes without saying
that you should never have
more children than you
have car windows.

ERMA BOMBECK

Biology is the least
of what makes
someone a mother.

**OPRAH WINFREY**

Children reinvent
your world for you.

SUSAN SARANDON

Like star dust glistening on fairies' wings, little girls dreams are of magical things.

SHERRY LARSON

A baby is sunshine and
moonbeams and more,
brightening your world
as never before.

ANONYMOUS

# In every girl
# is a goddess.

FRANCESCA LIA BLOCK

Wherever you go,
go with all
your heart.

CONFUCIUS

May you live every
day of your life.

JONATHAN SWIFT

**Rejoice with
your family in the
beautiful land of life.**

ALBERT EINSTEIN

The quickest way for a
parent to get a child's
attention is to sit down
and look comfortable.

LANE OLINGHOUSE

What a difference
it makes to come
home to a child.

MARGARET FULLER

THE FAMILY
IS ONE OF
NATURE'S
MASTERPIECES.

GEORGE SANTAYANA

It's extraordinary
to look into a baby's
face and see a piece
of your flesh and
your spirit.

**LIAM NEESON**

**A person's a person,
no matter how small!**

DR SEUSS

I'd walk through fire for my daughter. Well not FIRE, because it's dangerous. But a super-humid room.

RYAN REYNOLDS

The family you come from
isn't as important as the
family you're going to have.

RING LARDNER

Children are not things
to be moulded, but are
people to be unfolded.

JESS LAIR

# Family is the most important thing in the world.

PRINCESS DIANA

WE MADE A
WISH AND
YOU CAME
TRUE.

ANONYMOUS

If you're interested in finding out more about our books, find us on Facebook at Summersdale Publishers and follow us on Twitter at @Summersdale.

www.summersdale.com

IMAGE CREDITS

Cover images © LeonART l, monbibi,
Keep Calm and Vector/Shutterstock.com
Striped background © LeonART l/Shutterstock.com
Dotted background © monbibi/Shutterstock.com
Elephant © monbibi/Shutterstock.com
Stork © LeonART l/Shutterstock.com
Footprints © LeonART l/Shutterstock.com
Crown © Alona Syplyak/Shutterstock.com
Whales © monbibi/Shutterstock.com